HEADUGU

Selected Poems

SEAN OVA

All rights reserved.

No part of this publication may be translated, reproduced, or transmitted in any form or by any means, in whole or in part, electronic or mechanical including photocopying, recording, or by any information storage or retrieval system without prior permission in writing from the author.

The views expressed in this work are solely those of the author and do not necessarily reflect the views of the publisher, and the publisher hereby disclaims any responsibility for them.

Text copyright © Sean Ova

Cover Illustration copyright © Sean Ova

First Edition: April, 2018

The moral right of the author has been asserted.

Published by JDT Publications
Port Moresby, National Capital District, Papua New Guinea
Email: jdtpublications@gmail.com

National Library of Papua New Guinea
Cataloguing-in-Publication entry:

Ova, Sean. 1978 — .
    Headugu: Selected Poems.

    ISBN-13: 978-9980-901-60-6

    1. Poetry, Papua New Guinea. 1. Collected Works
PNG/821-dc 22

Printed in USA by CreateSpace Independent Publishing.

Arave oa Michael Aori Ovakora tau hinau Doris Boneku Ovakora.

Both God-fearing beyond the manifestations of language or thought.
Pray, this arrow flung flies far and from the bow of diversity.
And concentric ripples from the right wind… free us from these interminable storms. Take us to destiny.

Never shedding tears of compassion,
Neither nursing wounds of the past
Nor anticipating the forecast of tomorrow.

But bring fort a refuge! Those we who were once a drop of rain, a cell, (who fell from the sky) are no more caged.

And now make sustenance through existence, blow a flame for a million tribes, seek not prestige but impact a legacy. and once more… restore a sense of place.

With so much thanks to the following people who had the understanding for me in the span of over five years in getting to the bottom of this book;

Douglas Ova for the areas with word publishing I had no idea about in the first place and my Dad, Michael Ova, to whom valuable assistance for making available certain resources; human and technical. To Mum, who taught me about persistence, honour and the title of this compilation.

To my senior, Segeben, for the encouragement in the initial stages of this work. Michael K. my lecturer at UoG gave me a fair amount of courage as an experienced writer when I was still figuring out how to go about my anthology.

My sister, Gabby for the idea to compile an anthology. Because I persisted in bothering her with a pile of uncut poems in those early days at the University of Goroka.

My in-service colleagues back in 2003-4; (William Teka, Tony Kludapalo, Ruben Ere 'ere and Roselyn Toni) for their precious time to read some of my poems and give valuable feedback on better approaches.

Thank you to Jordan Dean for his decisive efforts and consistency towards the outlook and editions in this anthology. The energy invested in this work is surely God-sent.

Those many others who I may have forgotten in one way or another who gave me a hand in some step of the way. I hope I do not offend you if I may have overlooked your meaningful contribution in some way.

Finally, my fair wife Bina. Our precious children; Avoa-Yamuru Odette and Ivan-Ori Mundi Ova, Nick Ova and Robi Sean Ova Jnr. for an admirable amount of unlimited trust and patience, when I was away working on the manuscript. I hope one day you do understand - I owe you my world, the very one I write about.

CONTENTS

Headugu 9

Change 10

Samarai Pearlie Curlies 11

Night Man 12

Neo Misima 13

Jungle Bilum 14

Black Apollo 16

MOsKiTOiSM 17

Black Fire 18

Blue Extroverts 21

Streams of Green 22

Womb-Man 23

Melanesian Pearl 25

Public Motors 27

Sandwiched 28

Backyard Auction 29

Colour of Unity 31

Iki Ore 32

Nocturnal Kisses 34

Flaming Words	35
Outrigger Dugout of Yeli	37
Bilas Dinau	38
Hey Man: Your Stand	40
Heart in Hand	42
Bond of Infinity	44
Mister Wantok in a Neck Tie	46
The Ladder of Greed	47
Civilized Criminal	49
News and Views	50
Living Past	51
Land of the Unpredictable	53
Fences and Gates	55
Sailing Moth	56
Bit for Bite	56
Wet Spell on Sun City	56
Insanity	57
Water Dome of the Coral Sea	57
Calcium Grain	57

FOREWORD

Headugu, in the author's native language is the act of a fisherman seating in a canoe and lost in thought as his fishing line is cast into the sea. It is used metaphorically to mean waiting in anticipation for that great poem to be reeled in.

Through the use of strong imagery, the author explores his heritage to find meaning to everyday issues and exposes social inequalities. The poems present local contexts, attitudes and also legendary explanations to some of the dilemmas we face in life.

Teaching in rural schools in Papua New Guinea, the author makes various observations as he goes about his daily activities. He expresses his thoughts and views with passion. Philosophical questions are treated in a sarcastic way so that readers are entertained beautifully.

The anthology is filled with joy, lined with heart felt questions, marked with pain and will take you on a poetic journey.

Headugu is a vibrant addition to the growing collection of contemporary PNG literature. Well done Sean!

Happy reading.

Jordan Dean
Poet & Author of *Tama'gega – Fatherless Child*

SEAN OVA

HEADUGU

Addictive with words
Flavored with words
Coloured with words
Preserved in symbolism.

Tools prepared and stirred
To deliver bondage of a fugitive mind.

Feeding and fueling pages on a foolscap
By the runny tongue of a man who escapes
O'er dreamy soul – scapes and steel – scapes
nestling humanity in a sanctuary
Beyond gates of a cemetery
And frames within a painting
Breaking fences and opening doors
Of a drowning paradise.

Healing the eye sore
Surfing the sky over sweaty lips
Protruding over the calm – *Headugu*[1]
Bursting a rooftop like the punishing blade that spew
The feigning pompous in blood hands.

Liberated letters like footprints
On the vast sands of an erratic beach
Where the distant waves efface my footmarks
From memory but never the grain of sand
With one for every twinkling star.

---

[1] Headugu: The act of a fisherman seating in a canoe and lost thought as his fishing line is cast into the sea. It is used metaphorically to mean waiting in anticipation for that great poem to be reeled in.

CHANGE

Even a room of dust and cobwebs
A stagnant pool in some swamp
And the mangrove at low tide
Or a stuffy boys dormitory
A pig sty
Long the force of a naive breeze.

For creativity evokes
A change into office better than expensive air cons
A touch of class to quicken a slow hand
And a taste of beguilement in a village university
Some human ventilation system may be a welcome sight
How else do you clean the inside out?
Whatever corrupts?
Disrupts and
Then erupts
Ka …..BOOM!
Look at the bright side
The eye of a pen
Never lies.

SAMARAI PEARLIE CURLIES

Southern Samarai skies dwell many pearlies
Spread atop them bronzy faces
Who bore chacoaly, blacky curlies
Depicting grannies of them race.

When they walkabout, these things hang anyhow
Samashy, some are how some look spy no care
Anna me fighting to bear
This game I think it no fair.

The sun wake properly in the air
And coconut oil my stomach it stir
Round and round till me smile and stare
At hers *delisis*[2] flesh softy bare.

She laugh rough 'un and in me one flare
Fire like *diapani*[3] bomb here to tear
My black heart if I dare
To touch the sistas greasy hair.

Bara! Me like it to share
Them shaggy *kowakowa*[4] you wear
Prouding them woolly – noolly; for spare?
Bang! Catch you my Samarai magic glare.

Feel it, drink it spearing you there
Not will I forget in no – no years, you hear
Hair, bone and meat; I swear
Oledi I win before you sees me here
Because me note you aware
One point for the underwear.

---

[2] Delisis: Delicious (escape from using the common) yet noticeable.
[3] Diapani: Tawala dialectical pronunciation for 'Japanese'.
[4] Kowakowa: Misima island word for 'hair on the head'. Implied to the hair of a girl.

NIGHT MAN

As silent as a bat
On a dark night, imitating a deaf thief
In no hurry at all
And most wide awake
Than the moon
Waiting –
Night man.

Neo Misima

A site like dynamite for a smoke
Or a smile with a broken tooth
Vomiting gold into a flush toilet
Before those hey days; before nights of roots
Of royalties, feasts and splashing gay
Before the rush, the hush, the crush
All stainless steel glimmer of mercury
The wharf, the sand and back bending
Soil muddied water ways the departure
The bargain, the gain and the pain then the price shoot dead
Cold like hair rise feasting on germ shit, and the same peers
Who now have empty pockets and jeer
My stranger who recoils at their despise
Ancient homes with fire-extinguished landlords
Who shelter collecting *short necks*[5]
What the heck? Left for yesterday's speck
O Misima, O dear!

---

[5] Short necks: Refers to alcohol or booze. Common in PNG for the SP Lager short brown bottles.

JUNGLE BILUM

I.
Lushy ever green mother
My tranquil most; virgin ghost
Drenched with torment
We turn towards one another shivering
And reliving every hidden moment
Our beings nurture to be
In bounty and emptiness to be
The attire of tropical adornment
Wood eaters long your goodness fast
As if your flesh of worthless dust
Whatever lasts the earth must.

II.
My taker maker 'n' wazzi shaker
Blessed now I proceed dressed
To oust those wood thieves of your sisterly nature
Like a restaurant waiter
At some corner of this nation
Worn and pressed for granted
So be there no more shades
By your towering glades
To kneel and lie on your root like laps
Entering imperturbability relapses.

III.
Retrospective of the *bilum*[6] days; swinging
Your call and the voice scenting the breeze where echoes
Of deep murmurings like drones hide the shouts
Of groaning branches among the soft sensual soul
Out from a concrete shell
Sponging up decayed leaves aroma
Embedded by layers of honest age

---

[6] Bilum: String Bag

I grind seditious words on *Yesu's*[7] platform and
Spit them down at gods who pauperize
And well know it off by art; even the night grows eyes
See what by–products they sell imported
From the warehouse of hell.

IV.
In sworn acquiescence of my solitudes
Yoddling over mountain ranges
Bubbling in and over the sea, the swamps
And savannah of this thriving heartland
Weary to islands of the north and east wing
Bleeding the sap of Melanesian consciousness
Through jungles of enigmatic ancient civilizations.

V.
My jungle abode of vast symphony
From waterfalls, hot springs, caves
And stained soils – an ebb of living
Bursting my pride in innocence
Like a ruptured blood vessel
Emptying rivers dry; so I die crying
Afloat in a flood of stench mud
Budding yet cold roots are
Groping for my buried past
To make tribal towers from the ruin
And see fountains that erode steel mountains
Like a bowel of sugar melting in contact with water.

---

[7] Yesu: Jesus Christ

BLACK APOLLO

When I put on the tie they call it etiquette
When I eat with knife and fork
They call it table manners.

When I speak my vernacular
They call it uncivilized
When they kill trees for documentation
They call it preservation.

When I empty out my nostrils they call it filthy
When they do likewise and hanker chief it
They call it healthy.

When I call on my father's fathers
They call it demonic
When they say their petitions they call it prayer.

When I'm in full traditional splendor
They call it primitive
When they exhibit live nudity
They call it exotic dancing.

When they category a higher living standard
They call it wealth
When I try on the same for size
They categorize me the third world kind.

When I die the native way
There is a free resting space
When I die like them
The morgue is crowded.

When I call Papua New Guinea simply home
They call it absolute PARA-NICE.

MOsKiTOiSM
(FoR ThE masses LeD By a fEw.)

fLOKIN' LoN De sWaoMP KaMINaUt Ov YEstaDeI RaIns,
LaIk RiGgliN' LAvA IN a Si Ov saN
FeTlAnD 'n' ViCiSus
PlAnDeRiN' As DisRtaCTiVe PeSt
Iz der Got Pesticide FO MoSqUiToism.

oRiGiOnoLs Ov dE jANgOlS, PuFf'd
WiD StOloN BlAd;
De mAdAs wAsIm dIs SaIm GrAuN WId.

aKtivLy sAkIn Ap der OaN kAiN
MaS Be En uleGiSLaT'D Bil Ov Da tAMbARan hAus
"Go IN Tin, KAm aUt Fet."

Nu wAnS taEKoVa …sAiM ol storI
DeMoCrATiC mOsQuItOism . dInAU BlUt WOneM, mI
BlUt bEnk Huh? mIpElA SaVe , diS Gaim Ov yOrz IZ No
MoSqUiTo bItE! wEiA KeN De mElO marN HAId? Face
Id – Mi YO bLad BenK, Man!
A NoTiC Rids:
"TaeK kava: Ol WaNtOk,
SKiNNY RiLaKt-AnT dOnOrS wANTed
asK mOsquItoS IN BlaCk anD WHiTe
Are bOrN from MosQuitOs.

Black Fire

Amongst my filed brooding silences
Hidden away safe
There's nothing innovative to craft
But scream with a pen; who contains passage to my thoughts
What's my reward for jogging down a crowded street
Of whisperings and citrus truths?
Do you hear the voice somewhere inside
From nowhere near what I hear?
I gleam in sweat but nobody gives a glass of water.

I cry thirty three year old tears
From eyes that have been
Staring ahead for 50, 000 years
I look like a darling who
Drinks fish broth from this very South seas
I shimmer with rippling muscles
In the strength of 105 men (one being a woman)
Or is it too many less?

I have our anthem to sing, but it seems out of harmony
If only our lyrics are the sweat
Aptitude touch of honey that can
Heal broken homes in Bougainville.

The streaming tears of this flood rushes on and tramples
On the tiny toes of pregnant men
These will move the most stubborn
Of stones on a hopeless river bed
Toward the selfish mouth of the impatient Fly River
Waiting and groaning to swallow
Every single sand grain from the sediments
Of our deep birth land who continues sowing lost tongues.

I seek not the sand to trudge
Lest it fail to hold my infant toe marks.

I seek every gold nugget not
This land serves like an wanting dish
Lest it be stolen or kidnapped elsewhere
I seek no hilariously ironic image from a digital camera
Exposing what can be seen outside
Rather I should like to capture whatever that is within.

It might as well be wishing the maker
Had them made to turn clockwise in the first place
I won't take the hand shake gladly
If our hands cannot be glued for all time
Instead I would take the hand of the aborted child
Who shall never breathe in my own and write with
If there is a hornets nest to shake
I want the both of us to run off
In one direction and never apart
I want to walk tall, but succeed being waterproof
Like a taro leaf who shelters you my dear
From the spread of AIDS
I still want you to stroll by my side in the twilight of moon
Glow so that every coconut frond
Shall applaud the blaze of our black fire
We want to see black hands clap
And red betel nut filled mouths
Cheer madly like devoted fanatics
In a Blues and Maroons game
Just out from a hypnotic attack.

Bring the frangipani
Paint the outsiders sun glasses grey
See the fine flowers as good as decay
Strum the guitar do the *peroveta*[8]
How unaccustomed like a scrapped coconut shell
Than when it is with the white flesh
In a jiggered ocean of their civilization

---

[8] Peroveta: Local hyms

What titles of tarnishing tales of the east by the worst.

Now that the flame burns
We dance whichever way we choose
Without roasted feet like our brothers.

In the Bainings of West New Britain
Then we would speak a language of fire without
Burning each other anywhere below the throat
Like the Tolai sons do in all steam, sparks and awe
Yet set loose, a bird of glory arm in arm
Like the dancing daughters of Finschhafen on an island
'spilling coconut milk and honey' to a Pacific glory.

Blue Extroverts

Men in blue who comb the city
Like lice on a keratinous head.

They bug the libertine
Like flies, blue flies
On decaying malevolent
Street ways and suburbs.

Come pessimists
Knock, knock objectionable
Meet the force and of course
Be game; since losers are choosers.

Any corner, any loner or by goner
Any mourner any time.

In alarm of any of the call
Or the terror stricken cry
No one is above the law
Just feel your own way in the dark
Tapping the hairs on the back.

Mr. Kleptomaniac, Mr. Miscreant
This is no drill
Nor for the Mr. Universe title nor Logohu medal.

Being cuffed
Being stuffed in bandages
Or be handed to the head warden
Or worse, the undertaker.

Still – any blue fanatic?

The little boy who shares the same roof
With the man who uses a gun at work count.

STREAMS OF GREEN
(In the name of greenamony).

Over the rugged range of mounds
Rises a swollen wound
Breathless – expecting a bad ending
Within which, throbbing arteries
Pipeline the green juice
Coating feather embryos, every beginnings
Under incubation and submissive embrace
Unlegislated to let live, what breathes.

Here she oversees, she provides
In jungle murmuring milk resoviours
For every vein in flora, none forgotten
Artery in fauna, her congealing rays of light
Penetrates the rainforest canopy
Bathing the pores of green streams
To applaud; to respond instinctively by intuition
Until the upright, the tailless know – it all
Casts suffocating shadows
Blasting dynamite like the delivery in haste
And band aid artificial recovery.

Tsk…tsk…tsk to take away from
Her is to melt icing of green cream;
Like the egg of her womb, robbed in blind pity
Leaving what used to be a stomach into an ancient tomb
A habitat into a bald patch of infertile dust
Lost in the spoils of sport.

WOMB-MAN

I'm just a string in the *bilum*
The ping of marital asylum
The *sinebada*[9] in the shadow
An item flung out the window.

I'm the water in the rain
The medicine for your pain
The lead on your line and mine
Is cast to buy me some thyme.

I'm the victim of bigamy
Public shown of afro–cifica and home grown
The hard earner, breadwinner; all weathered gardener
Whose hands, hold seeds, get sown when thrown.

I'm the sparkle in the eye
The twinkle in your day to day sky
The moonlight at night
When a hot bed flames alight.

I'm the tears of a frigid room
The fears in rushing too soon
The cockerel who rises early
To prepare your meals surely.

I'm blinded by the jealous wind
The blinded kind hard to find
Your kindred of an open mind
When silhouettes and ghosts haunt my kind.

I'm the kindle of the candle,
No firewood bundle I cannot handle.

---

[9] Sinebada: Lady or woman

SEAN OVA

The child bearer to wear your name
And the pair of legs to walk your shame.

I'm the cage basket some ribs less
Even the maker overlooked my muscled mess
But the source and springing life force
Born right yet ill–willed, of course.

I'm the beat of the melancholic drum
Worn out from loneliness of 'the bum'
Who received a shower of lullabies from his mum
Now old, feel the cold of what is to come.

I tire this race off from all the noise
And wait to claim my long awaited due
Build a monument to teach young boys
And those who call themselves 'men' to stay true.

MELANESIAN PEARL
(To all Melanesia).

From phantoms in the vast pacific ocean
A girl, a dark mama, my Melanesian pearl
Centuries rippled to the wail of the conch
When countless voyages of barter proceeded
Launch after launch sharing dreams
From father to son, mother to daughter
The orals of a voice with knowing ears
Longing to the seas noise
Seasonal monsoons, well wishes and tropical dishes
At the seaside swept winds of harvesting fishes
Reading the sun, the moon and the sea hawk
Up high ward spanning round ceremonial clock.

A passion in the soil, through its healing oil
Where the barrier of many tongues outlasts any trade
And words fade and bargains of honour made
Belief and myth of a market in Melanesian words
Warriors, peacemakers, sorcerers, borne lords
To live the way her people seen to his day
And listened to the darkness of evil nights' say.

Chasing the black man's needs
Written in hearts of enchanted creeds
Defying pathetic wind and tide of changes
From the white west, moaning above strange hilly ranges
Leaving no room for my ethnic civilizations
Would I have equaled other nations
Like them Aztecs, Egyptians or Greek
One may never know slow rivers from deep creeks.

My *bubu mama*[10] is never lost in scandalism
In this rough ocean of cultural vandalism.

---
[10] Bubu mama: Grand mother

She smiled with children she cuddles
Who paddle a multitude of crushing hurdles.

Saying: "Unless my black *blut*[11] you spill
My woman child, pass on an omen of ill–will."

---

[11] Blut: Blood

Public Motors

Increase, bus fare
Bus route, decrease
Accelerate
Black smoke, heart stroke
Escalate rate
No joke, you choke
Cut short, life span
People, road ants
Week commuter
Rush in rodents
Owner, donor
Morgue on rust wheels
No rego – speed up
Going – coming
Install'd, barb'd seats
Do tear clothing
Or bleed your meat
Road worthiness
Load warriors
Leave days filth
Seat belt health
Stray dogs' death
On stilts
Safety, service
Crew slack, eye sore
Public transport Private comfort?
Peep, peep – don sleep
NLTB [12]
What's it to be?

---

[12] NLTB: National Land Transport Board

Sandwiched
(For all the hard working teachers in PNG).

An eight to – four o – six public servant
Crawling uphill and shouldering
Massive outcomes like an ant
Bridging the urban with the rural.

Can't have the last laugh
I'm used and confused
When the smoking chalk dust is defused.

A degree holder, never any bolder
But already feeling a hundred years older.

Over driven with schedules each working day
And out smarted by king – size dues to pay.

Over ridden with paper work
I miss the taste of costly pork at the end of a kitchen fork.

I know I'm being over used
But refuse to feel confused.
Call it sandwich abuse or misuse
From both sides in and lavishly accused.

I'd like to sit still by my passing traditions
But break out into hot sprint for my ambitions
Mr. Employer at Waigani presses buttons to key deductions.

I co – operate in order to get squeezed
Somebody better hope I don't get pissed.

BACKYARD AUCTION
(Sold – integrity of the state).

Going for K100.
'Kilim em. Wantok bilong husait'?
Tribal fighting conduces ingredients
To a blood cake. Shot by one
Countryman served severely severed
Tok e dai! Ol indai.

Going for K50.
Tok pisin, the new voice
Official no-choice language: 'english'
Eight hundred languages and counting down
Language loss ain't a crime, at least not ever!
Tok pinis
Going fifth!

Going for K40.
Firewood for sale! Surprise, surprise! in PNG?
Wood to cook food: take it or leave it?
Nothing is free
Going forth!

Going for K30.
Darts at Kakaruk market
Kam winnim bia – olgeta wokim tu yah!
Going thrice!

Going for K20.
Stain clothed and scruffy
Through the supermarket exit
Frisked: Beep! Beep!
Opps! On the pubic forbidden
Sarrup: company policy
Going twice!

Going for K10.
A mere child aged ten
On the ATM line – pay him
Only to speed up your banking queue
Going once!

Colour of Unity

White brain –
Salt of the earth gain dry bare feet gulp up the rain
Silenced voices complain pain twice in vain.

Black heart –
Our first heritage, a land teeming milk and honey for a start
Into a people gifted for the Melanesian works of art
Lost patriotic hands into educated fools' gold chasing
centuries apart.

Red blood –
With rainbow umbrellas from floods
We wade on neck deep in a quick sand of chocolate mud
Uprooting grassroots and every nerve of your soul
To make flower buds.

IKI ORE[13]

She soaks the sun at dusk
So within we long much to ask
She deliveries from crevices, pristine waters
So within our lungs the world wind enters
Her thoughts of our space in silence
So within we pride a careless abundance
Failing to feel within, wails the heart within.

She wears the aroma of an arm in arm friend
So we long graves of red that bring us an end
She dwells in the wings of the dove
So within raindrops we sip tears made from above
Yet some roamer got his placard up as the best
On how to slit her throat wide open in ways of the west.

When the seedlings' eye turn blind red
Within we bite each other at the head
She whooping coughs fetid sewage
So within dreamt up luxury; the swamp of garbage
She sleeps behind open walls dreading garrulous jets zooming
So within every room we build
Catastrophe and havoc is looming.

Yearning material earning, our persistence ignores learning
She plants the devils right on her laps of ice
So within we are embroiled in despise
She bores steel deep within down into her womb
So within edges the holocaust of gas or bomb
She remains our life, our do – it yourself grave
So within her affinity we need crave
Sailors sailing canoe with holes on board
Tire the fire in bailing hands on board.

---

[13] Iki ore: The heart knowing or way of knowing in Ihu dialect, Miha area, Gulf Province

Her emotions in us evolve in harmony
While hand chest resting glint the sparkle
As you see silver in the eye of a child chuckle
And hear someplace deep within hearts of ebony.

NOCTURNAL KISSES

Some people have one each night
To share their mosquito net with
Some have two
I had all six at one time last night!
Boy! Did they have the time of their lives
Kissing me all over hungrily
So every inch of my naked torso and limbs
Received full attention
If it wasn't for my shorts kept on
My middle front and middle back zones
Would not be safe!
I was useless, hopeless and senseless
What choice did I have for
I was outnumbered. Six to one!
With eyes shut, every-time they pumped
Away at me all night long, robbing me
Off much needed sleep 'til the break of dawn
When I finally had both eyes open
I saw them satisfied beyond enough
Yet something told me they
Wanted to bug me for more
So I gave each a mighty clap
When I opened my clasped palms
The bloody mosquitoes were no more.

Flaming Words

I saw a man speak with flaming words
A girl who gave birth to poetry
When it grew –

They shed skin from black and white
Into an awesome rainbow
Crimson, sapphire and ochre
And I saw the water turn into cordial.

When the words pierced a child
He saw energy become flesh and blood.

When poetry rested in a lady's blossom
She sang a strange tune and flowers bloomed
As they were dispelled from her lips
He couldn't depart. Never.

When a widow covered it in a mourning cloth
It became glossy velvet and regal ashes.

When the orphan walked on the soil
Every step he went a sprungle rapidly.

When a teacher wrote on the board
The chalkboard transformed like a mirror on the wall
And the pupils saw a hidden route unveiled.

When the preacher spoke at his sermon
The light and the wind flew in together
and darkness ran out the window in shame.

When the politician touched his documents
And signed on their behalf the district wept
Tears of unity.

All of a sudden things could talk
And sing and even think and dance.

Outrigger Dugout of Yeli

Like a dugout from the far, far eastern ways
Beyond bleached sands of the 'Calvados chain'
You who was carved from clay to coil my days
While many things happen below the great Jinjo skies.

A child who ate from the charcoal fires and its realities
The great one whom we were destined for many things
So we could learn from the mistakes and abilities giving
Our tired paddling arms mysterious wings.

What more do I desire on this little fishing trip
As our canoe budges through strange waters in folklore
Pressing our informed minds to take a flexible grip
As we hurl onboard hybrid fishes never seen before.

Here love dove – enter in a sacred coral cove
When huge waves threaten our hearts and things might stop
Pray we this gloomy seas for help from up above
To shower down a silent foam over their blown rooftops.

Our voyage only has begun, in both deep and shallow
Waters streaming to and from our labors
Time rocks and slogs as we must follow
This good ole dugout into our one true homely harbor.

BILAS DINAU

Ol wantok mi singaut – harim
Lo lusim go lo laik, bai no e-nap karim.

Sin bilong you mi kisim
Lotu bilong yu mi misim
Ron bilong yu mi bekim
Graid bilong mi failim barata Jisas mi nilim
Hevi blo husait mi pilim.

Papa pikinni blo narapela –
Arapela mi lokim long haus kalabus
Em wantok yet, laka!
Pikinini bilong yu mi givim kaikai
Guinea pik bilong yu mi banisim
Chok dus kirap nating yu pinisim.

Mi yet mi bilasim wantaim hap hap
Oslem karamap haitim samtin wantaim lap lap.

Tru! Tru! Hevi e narakain
Mi laik shadoim yu, natin tasol
Noggat hevi kamapim bel kol long dinau
Olsem dok singaut taim em lukim shadow
Tasol man tru we?

Ol lain blo yu mi singautim
Lain bilong ol lus nating
Mi kisim taim Lo sik bilong yu
Na kaikai bilong yu.

Mi marit na ring blo yu mi bilasim.

Spear blo mi stap lo museum blo yu
Gun blo yu mi holim na blut I kapsait Lo han bilong mi.

Pis lo solwara mi wasman
Gavman kisim mit na bun
Yu tromoi e kam.

Stori bilong mi yu holim
Pasin tumbuna bilong mi
Yu raitim blo ol lain blo yu.

Na mi yu mas banisim long lek e go antep long het
Lo bilasim yu yet.

Dinau stap olsem bilas
Yu skelim hevi na mi yet tasol bai pilim
Na pulim e go e kam.

HEY MAN: YOUR STAND

I.
Kati (male voice)

Almighty dondon, for your sake in love
Into your hand may my wawu land
Fly of me white wings of your giant dove
As silence and struggle tussle my wait
For it is your fist that now grasps of me fate
In this calamity and woman wanting state
Here I'm; awake – a go at my turn
From rude waters, which I yearn to learn
The full warmth from your glowing face
The rush of the flesh and beauty at the base.

II.
I neither beg nor brag lord *bubu*[14]; mould the clay
Within her womb, even there passively lay
So it bloom out from this shadows of gloom
And mayest bypass this darkness of doom
Lessen the burden, thus she not sadden
Though, it may be seen to have her overridden
A path of jiggered stones unturned her lover hidden
Despite many unspoken trials and wistful errors
I share this first timers anguish and feminine terrors.

III.
Speak fort the language of each passing wave to disciples
Washed in fear above lake Galilee's brave
When crashing up against M.V John Vincent
And seal every leak of its ribs and hull from decent
My raft on dreams reveal the carver of his craft
Captain of the seafarers to you I kneel confined
In your designs of my belief, I send this poem

---

[14] Bubu: Grandparent or ancestor

Relief shaken, I'd swim this boisterous sea with my bare
Hands and claw in air to view her face again
If it means to ask of me more agony and pain
I willingly do not mind a few drops of red stain
Straining all odds and extremes beyond every man's standing.

Heart in Hand

I.
Wawu (feminine voice responds)

Don don of love, who watches from above
Bring him Kati; me loves for my being starves
As he sails these sinister sister seas
Please, please, ease these breath of peace-breeze
So that my lost heart may just kiss his
Standing entwined I shan't miss
Of him every seducing enticing piece.

II.
Vile marine fury of the south westerly
How this joy swells me
Gluing our bloods be
Right there, soothing this fears
Father in your palms, my tempting tearing tears
So shall he triumph to this tender heart beat
Our feet and our chattering teeth greet
Come home, hum home to roam my passion
As my flesh melts softly in rocking chair fashion
Sour hours away from your power, for all times sake
Out of this genuine make – here's yours to take
These seed flesh throbbing my feminine lake.

III.
Now, now hear my ear stink with singing ringing
O how my Kati love sings of glee-free things
I'm entirely yours just as you are settling scores
On pain shift tides where the spirit rides
There by your hip sides till shadows my eye hides
It matters to cut the ribbon and finally declare
My desire steep intension, my soul stripped bare.

To you I do dare, for I care
Here's proof for you my awful, awful favor
Wanna be employed full – time neighbor?
Cash and Carry my hour upon hour labor.

Bond of Infinity

I.
Kati of a masculine voice: "Stone catcher"

Barriers of stone some men make
Another only snakes
One then hurls at, another catches
To fall or stand sweats freedom, a sorrow to soar
For what is tomorrow rich with any way?

Its aberration hallucinations and sacred
Acres of pandemonium. But fare on forth
With scars of pride. reach my hand
And yours too, love bound homebound
Wawu and your engulfing charms
Have my arms bound and my tongue gagged
Now a captive of sweet – life sentence
Hospitalised for a tipped passion poisoned arrow
Living on a drip of your charisma and charm from a chest
that heaves and falls for you.

II.
Wawu – Ferminine voice: Crystal night.

Kati my moonlight; my never ending song
My soul alight streams right, all along tonight
You being my grave choice
Sends me the echo of your brave voice
Sparks streaks of gold light
Jetting upon first sight a dim narrow plight
Calm over ripples and smooth reflections
Penetrate deep affections and a dead
Reaction of interactions fusing hot sweet attraction
Ever sparkling fractious speculation and complication
Of paternal contradiction to you still
And ever my moonlit conviction.

III.
Duet: Rainbow True.

Embrace me now, the only way you know how
On your marks get set me on this sweet race
We barefoot it on the sun's face
Let our story glow in the in–law show
These coconut madness glory
Without you futile without me
As in you embellishes me
On a path narrow; our ravenous arrow
Speeding away raucously on oceans blue
In search of the arc – rainbow hue
To love you too, is sweet home coming true.

Mister Wantok[15] in a Neck Tie

Hear, hear, my people – my words in ink
For all; whoever big or small, me think!
'bout this a cycle of vain due to a bunch of banana sons
Man driving, soul drawing the others to the brink
Instead of indigenizing our livelihood
We assimilate into the dominant sub – culture
Instead of localizing those basic services
We centralize the multi - corporations
Instead of manipulating cash commodities
Appropriately; we welcome monopolic – money wallets
Instead of delivering public funds
We convert it into ghost figure (embezzlement).

In the end master neck – tie gets away on petty fines
An old philosophy states: "the neck – tie who points down
cruise around the affluent streets of town".

To you country men or not, your cronies and yes – men
I've had it to the brim. We'll all rot and our blood
The worms wriggle cheers a drink. But at least
I am no real drop out. At least, I am no tax – milker
At the very least – I'm no rapist of this motherland.

---

[15] Wantok: Tribesman/woman, of the same clan who speak the same language. Today, used to refer to all Melanesians.

THE LADDER OF GREED

No thirst too small
Secondhand ransom
Last to all
The best for some.

The want of 'we should'
And fast, fast food
Fashionable clothes
Fugitive thoughts indifferent deeds.

To being that fast being
A woman, or a girl
Needs to man the odds
Or else get man – handled
How naïve of the native?

When shall there be
A motherly man aching
To embrace childlike citizens
On the threshold of milk and honey.

The climb crime skidder like a skyscraper
Don't matter who you trample on
Don't count who be on top of your own species.

Just go about eradicating one blessing after another
In exchange for one curse for a new curse.

As mankind race for every need
He who reaches the top already
Puts on the shiny shield of greed.

See me
Envy me
For I'm the tallest of you all

SEAN OVA

Me, my – self, I – my!
When big men play dirty.

CIVILIZED CRIMINAL

Equality and then where?
Some permitted more allowance than others.

Education for all and then what?
Qualified outnumber the disqualified.

Employment and then where?
Cultural shift – language drift.

Urbanization and then what?
A class system of 'haves and have nots'

Positional hierarchy and then what?
Misconduct in office and circumlocution (red tape)
More policies/amendments and then what?
A little fee to bend steel rods of the law.

Free trade and then what?
Little handouts and fat interests
White markets and black markets.

Foreign aid and then what?
The boomerang ritual/initiations.

The global village and then what?
First world, second world, third world, ??? world.

Whatever happened to the civil world?

News and Views

Radio, studio
Visual, usual
Disease – please ease
Misuse, amuse
Accused, excused!
Violence, no fence
Ambulance
Surveillance, free–lance
Silence: no offence!

Sport shot, hot spot
Further, weather
Broadcast, net cast
Internet, interpret
Code switch, mode switch
Program, problem.
Negative addictive
Advertise, scrutinize
By Whose eyes?
White lies, realise!
Money wise, how nice
Shallo' news, hollo' views
Interviews – sinister news.
North, south. Media shout
East, west
News out! Mouth bout
What about?

LIVING PAST
A matrilineal legend from Miyakewa.

Here in the lime light I am stiff
Grinning lime white in grief
No maybe no more and no if
For my pieces mark the fall of a fading field
My remains to the grass yield
Extinguishing the flame of my name
Where a clay pot; my cold head shield
To my final spear wounded Sariba soil
Fastening down my rough neck tame
And a sour stomach which over–boils
yearly I greet the eyes of the sky
But without blind of dear day or night
For your sake in matrilineal dust now I lie
For whom the Hehego cry:

Ap ega tam, ap ega tiyai geka![16]

Gardening the *miyakewa*[17] and my
Stolen bride known as Sariba's pride
In empty grimace and sleep deep
Care taking this island sheep
When day pass along I blend
From flesh to crust, crust to dust
In eternal smile, dreaming endless miles
And a will to make a must
That one day bursts rust just fast and hailed
Soiled hero of the *Hehego*[18]
Rest now saint in *Kwabunamoa*[19] quest spearhead

---

[16] Ap ega tam, ap ega tiyai geka!: *Bohilai Tawala* translation – If it wasn't for you, it wouldn't be for us!) Implied appreciation on behalf of my Hehego tribe.
[17] Miyakewa: Traditional or ancestral name for Sideia Island. Bwanabwana/Samarai group of Islands, Milne Bay Province.
[18] Hehego: My native (maternal) clan name. Sideia Island -Bohilai Tawala speaking society.

Of my generation and the next
Come forward as I preserve your bone marrow.

Listen as we load words in the eye of the arrow
Tomorrow has come, may your spirit I borrow?

---

[19] Kwabunamoa: Ancestral name for the bay in which I define as home. Sideia Island, Milne Bay Province.

LAND OF THE UNPREDICTABLE

In the land of the unexpected…

Sounds of;
Drums beating, excited people meeting.
Happy feet stomping, while the bull toned *garamuts*[20] mourns
Enthusiastic vocal chords strained and shelled necklaces
Clatter in a language I feel at home to.

Smell of;
Mumu from an underground oven
Taro Mona[21] cooling on slow heat in a clay pot
Ginger blown as fragrance into the air
Duduna[22] over the coconut charcoaled fire.

Sight of;
Reefs below glow in an emerald sea is concealed
A smiling painted face to a complete foreigner
A carving on a wall
A dancer in sweat and coconut oil or pig fat
A elementary child singing and dancing to assure the old
Of maintaining his origins.

A touch of;
Loss and grief in a lament by the ancient orators voice plenty
to eat for everyone except the deceased
The bad grass pricking my bare feet
The first cries of a newborn in a shelter
A mother swaying a baby in a *bilum*[23] to sleep.

---

[20] Garamut: Hollowed wooden gong beaten with sticks.
[21] Taro mona: Native Milne Bayan equivalent to flour dumplings.
[22] Duduna: *Bohilai Tawala* word for mangrove mud shellfish. Often roasted over charcoal embers.
[23] Bilum: String Bag

Taste of;
Red fruit from Papua New Guinea's further east
Rossel Island and sushi gobbled as a native dish
Fresh fish out from the sea and into the pan.

FENCES AND GATES

Too much *karanas*[24] along the road
Too many potholes on the bitumen
Too many tombstones of colonialism
Too many mouths and short hands
Too many roosters crowing at a moonlight night
Too many boys who decorate the malfunctioning streetlamp
Too many men in skirts and bras
Too many crucifixes on the house of shadows
Too many KBEs, CGMs, CEOs, MOUs, MOAs and UFOs
Too many miles, when only a meter is enough
Too many fences with band–aid all over cut wire
Too many parrots who cannot teach me to fly
Too many gates and not that many spare keys
Too many pockets with broken stitches
Too many *wantoks*[25] who treasure your name on the beach
Too many girls who think with their scrotums.

---

[24] Karanas: Coral or limestone rocks.
[25] Wantoks: In PNG or all Melanesia, a term referring to same speaking kin.

Sailing Moth

Brown leaf from the bough
Did not quiver in the breeze
Sailed of faltering.

Bit for Bite

Trekking amid grass
Groping for food to store up
To me seen as crumbs.

Wet Spell on Sun City

Fierce sun, Pom city
Reluctant to be weaned off
From drained breast-like clouds.

INSANITY

The howling south west
Resurrects the sleeping sea
In teeth grit fury.

WATER DOME OF THE CORAL SEA

Sub world in crystal
Coral cities of rainbow
A dome like no dream.

CALCIUM GRAIN

Cheapest diamond glints
Shimmering white from each grain
In a spur of light.

ABOUT THE AUTHOR

Sean Ova was born on July 30, 1978 in Lae, Morobe Province, Papua New Guinea. He completed a Bachelor in Education from the University of Goroka and is currently undertaking a Masters in Creative Writing at the University of Sydney, Australia.

He has taught English at various primary and secondary schools in the National Capital District and Milne Bay Province. Sean is passionate about creative writing and wishes to see his work encourage others to write as well.

Sean is married to Balbina Nicholas and they have four awesome kids. They call Alotau, Milne Bay Province home.

www.ingramcontent.com/pod-product-compliance
Lightning Source LLC
Chambersburg PA
CBHW072034060426
42449CB00010BA/2256